12 ANGRY MEN

Reginald Rose

AUTHORED by Sean Peter Drohan
UPDATED AND REVISED by Elizabeth Weinbloom

COVER DESIGN by Table XI Partners LLC
COVER PHOTO by Olivia Verma and © 2005 GradeSaver, LLC

BOOK DESIGN by Table XI Partners LLC

Published by GradeSaver LLC, www.gradesaver.com

First published in the United States of America by GradeSaver LLC. 2012

GRADESAVER, the GradeSaver logo and the phrase "Getting you the grade since 1999" are registered trademarks of GradeSaver, LLC

ISBN 978-1-60259-291-9

Printed in the United States of America

For other products and additional information please visit
http://www.gradesaver.com

Table of Contents

Biography of Rose, Reginald (1920-2002)

Reginald Rose is most famous as a television writer, acclaimed for his teleplays in the "Golden Age" of television. Born and raised in New York City, he lived there until he enlisted during World War II, returning to pursue a career in writing.

Among other awards, Rose won three Emmys in his lifetime and was nominated for a total of six. Rose is most well-known for writing teleplays. However, he also found success writing for the stage, as well as for regular television programming.

Rose notably wrote teleplays for CBS's *Studio One*. Plays include 'The Bus to Nowhere,' '12:32 a.m.,' 'An Almanac of Liberty,' 'Crime in the Streets,' and 'Twelve Angry Men,' Rose's most known teleplay. 'Twelve Angry Men' continued to have a remarkable life as a landmark film, greatly expanded upon from the original teleplay, and a successful stage play.

Rose's plays are known for their direct handling of social problems and the political arena, uncharacteristic of a medium usually preoccupied with private, interpersonal relationships. Rose's work was unapologetic, confronting these issues directly.

While dealing with social issues, Rose was known as a master craftsman for television, as displayed by his incredible mastery of naturalism in this "slice of life" medium. *Twelve Angry Men's* success as a movie marked a major contribution of Rose and television for film, influencing the future of American cinematography.

About 12 Angry Men

12 Angry Men has had a long history of production and revision, from short teleplay to major Broadway productions. Reginald Rose first found inspiration for *12 Angry Men* when he served on a jury in a manslaughter case, over which the jurors fought bitterly for some eight hours. This became the impetus for the teleplay, *12 Angry Men*, which aired on CBS as a live one-hour drama. It was immediately successful and led to further development, culminating in its film version in 1957, starring Henry Fonda and directed by Sidney Lumet. It was first produced for the stage in 1964. It was filmed again for television in 1997, starring George C. Scott and Jack Lemmon, and first appeared on Broadway in 2004.

Dramatically, *12 Angry Men* is an excellent example of the mid-20th century American style of socially conscious, psychologically driven realism, depicting everyday individuals in everyday situations. In form, the play is a perfect piece of naturalism, occurring in real time and running continuously, even between acts, for the length of the drama.

Historically, we can look at the play in the context of its original film release date, 1957. The United States was in a politically transitional time. The Civil Rights Movement was well underway with the Brown vs. Board of Education decision passed in 1954 and the Montgomery Bus Boycott of 1956. Many of the themes of racial and social inequity being played out in the drama were being played out on the national scene.

Note: It is upon that 2004 Broadway script that this guide is based.

About 12 Angry Men

Character List

Foreman

The Foreman is responsible for keeping the jury organized, which is his main focus in the play. He is an assistant football coach outside of the jury room.

2nd Juror

A shy bank clerk who takes time to feel comfortable enough to participate in the discussion.

3rd Juror

3rd Juror is a small business owner. He proudly says that he started his business from scratch and now employs thirty-four workers. We learn early on that he has a bad relationship with his own son, with whom he is no longer speaking. We are led to believe that this is a contributing factor to his prejudice against the defendant, accused of stabbing his own father. 3rd Juror is the last to be convinced and only changes his mind once he realizes that he is only projecting his feelings about his own son onto the defendant.

4th Juror

4th Juror is a stock broker. He wears glasses and seems to handle himself with a very serious air. He deals with the facts of the case logically and concretely.

5th Juror

5th Juror works in a Harlem hospital and says that he himself has lived in the slums his entire life. This gives him insight into such details as the use of a switchblade.

6th Juror

A house painter, he is happy that the case continues as it means he doesn't have to work, but is hesitant to put a potential killer back on the streets. He sticks up for 9th Juror, an old man, and seems to be a respectful man.

7th Juror

7th Juror's main concern in the case is whether or not it will end before his ball game, for which he has tickets. He sells marmalade and is generally indifferent to the case. He changes his vote to "not guilty" simply because the tide of opinion switches, and he wants the deliberations to be over.

8th Juror

He is the only juror who votes "not guilty" at the first vote. He is discontent with the way the trial was handled and wants them to discuss the evidence in greater detail. Met with much opposition, he continues to advocate for the boy. We learn that he is an architect, by trade.

9th Juror

9th Juror is an old man. He respects 8th Juror's passion and sense of justice and quickly comes to his aid and becomes and advocate for the defendant.

10th Juror

He is one of the most fervent attackers of the defendant. Tactless and fairly bigoted, he condemns the defendant as "one of them" right from the start.

11th Juror

11th Juror is a German immigrant watchmaker. He is very patriotic and talks about how much he loves the American justice system.

12th Juror

12th Juror works for a marketing agency, to which job he refers to often. He seems constantly distracted from the case.

Major Themes

Justice

At the onset of the play, we learn from the Judge's offstage opening instructions the given circumstances of the play, that a man has been accused of murder and his fate is to be determined by these jurors. Immediately, we are launched into a world where the ultimate objective is to complete the "grave responsibility" of determining a man's innocence and guilt, the heart of the American justice system.

Throughout the play, we see two opposing views of justice. From 8th Juror and others, as they join, we see a perspective of justice that favors the accused and that wants most for him to have a fair shot. To 8th Juror, the boy's poor and troubled upbringing, his shoddy state-appointed defense attorney, and the jury's quick near-decisive decision to convict him are all gross forms of injustice.

Conversely, we see another side of justice proposed by the other members of the jury, who feel that the accused is clearly guilty, and anything other than conviction and execution is short of justice. 6th Juror articulates this most clearly, saying, "Suppose you talk us outta this and the kid really did knife his father?" This type of justice depends on retribution and vengeance. Rose plays off the two-sided nature of justice to create tension and contrast the characters. Each character wants "justice," but what justice becomes unclear and fluid throughout the course of the play.

Prejudice

Prejudice is observed on several levels throughout the course of the play. In the most obvious sense, the play deals with racial prejudice. While, conspicuously, the race of the accused is never certain, we do understand that he is a minority of some sort (in the 1957 film, the actor playing the accused was Italian), and this quickly becomes a heated issue among the jurors, especially for 9th Juror, who refers to the accused as "one of them."

Looking at prejudice in a larger sense, we find that, while maybe not racially driven, many of the jurors enter the jury room with preconceived notions and irrational ideas. 3rd Juror seems to be prejudiced against the accused simply because of his age, which seems to remind him of his estranged son. An interesting example of "reverse prejudice" is 8th Juror, who is initially sympathetic to the accused, not because of the evidence, but because he pitied his poor and troubled upbringing.

Doubt

What's really interesting about the case within *12 Angry Men* is that we never ultimately find out for sure whether the accused is guilty or innocent. While much of the evidence is aptly questioned and manipulated by 8th Juror, at the end of the case there remains a tremendous amount of evidence built up against the accused. Still, it is "beyond a reasonable doubt" that the jurors must find the accused guilty in order to convict him, and they all ultimately come to the conclusion that they have at least some doubt. We leave the play with a sense that justice and right has prevailed over irrationality and prejudice, but, pointedly so, we never actually find out the truth. This doubt over who is on the "right" side pervades the psychologies of the characters in the play and any audience watching.

One Against Many

The action of the play begins as 8th Juror votes 'not guilty' against 11 votes of 'guilty,' from the other jurors. This creates an immediate antagonism from the other jurors (10th Juror shouts, "Boy-oh-boy! There's always one"), and we quickly find that the task of our protagonist is to convince these eleven other jurors, which he slowly but surely does. This is framed as an act of bravery, standing up against the group to do what's right.

However, at the end of the play, there is a chilling reversal, as all of the jurors switch their vote to "not guilty," except for 3rd Juror, at which point 8th Juror points out, "It's eleven to one...you're alone." This moment is pointedly characterized contrarily as one stubborn man, refusing to come over to the side of reason. Rose contrasts these moments to provide a strong point of view for the play, as well as characterizing the two Jurors.

Class

The play proudly presents a tremendous cross-section of American life. The play juxtaposes a presumably wealthy stock broker (4th Juror) with someone who has admittedly lived in the slums his entire life (5th Juror), and we seem to have every level of working man in between. For many of the jurors, we have no more information than their occupation, which gives us an idea of socioeconomic level. These people are defined by what they do for a living. 7th Juror is even so tactless as to report his income of $28000, from selling marmalade, to the group.

Similarly, the idea of class in American society is brought to the forefront in the deliberation. 8th Juror immediately cites the boy's poor upbringing as a possible explanation for his juvenile criminal record and suggests that he has not been given adequate representation, due to his low social status. It calls into immediate question whether the American justice system is fair across classes.

Father/Son Relationships

It is very important to note that the defendant was accused of murdering his father. This relationship becomes very important in how 3rd Juror and 8th Juror understand the accused. Both identify over the play as fathers. 8th Juror exemplifies a somewhat paternal relationship with the accused, even though he doesn't know him and they are never seen together. He stands up for him in a very

Major Themes

paternal way and empathizes with the plight of his life.

Conversely, 8th Juror projects onto the accused his relationship with his own son, from whom he has been estranged for two years. The result is that 3rd Juror is immediately prejudiced against him. This play is in many ways a multi-generational play, featuring men of many different age groups; this coupled with the fact that the play is all-male definitely embeds the patriarchy of the times as well.

Anonymity

No names whatsoever and almost no specifics are used throughout the play. The jurors are simply referred to as a number, and the defendant is referred to as "defendant," "accused," "boy," etc. Even the witnesses are, "the downstairs neighbor," "the old man," etc. Ignoring the opening stage directions, there are no indications of time and place, except that it is summer and the fact that the play is all men - which does date it, but even that can (and has frequently) been changed in production.

The effect is that the play is not fixed. It could be the jury room of your trial or your neighbor's. It could be New York. It could be Wisconsin. The characters are less specific individuals and more of a general representation of the American population. These are everyday people that could very well be on your jury. This sense of anonymity raises the stakes of the play as a social drama, in that is a more general commentary on the American legal system.

Major Themes

Glossary of Terms

Abstain

Refrain from (in this case, voting).

Acquit

To find a defendant 'not guilty' of a charge.

Bigot

Someone who is intolerant of someone else's beliefs, opinions, race, ethnicity, or other differing characteristic.

Burden of proof

The requirement to prove one's own case over another. In America, the burden of proof is on the prosecution, meaning that they must prove their case beyond a reasonable doubt.

Coroner

One who examines a dead body.

Cross-examine

To question a witness called to testify for the other side.

Defendant

Someone who is charged with a crime and brought to trial.

Deliberate

To discuss the facts of a case and come to a conclusion or guilt or innocence.

Elevated Train

An above-ground public transportation train system.

Evidence

That which is used to prove a point or case (in a court of law).

Homicide

Murder

Hung Jury

When a jury cannot come to a unanimous decision, and the case must be retried in front of a new jury.

Premeditated

Planned or thought out.

Prosecutor

A lawyer who presents evidence in court to try to prove the defendant guilty.

Reasonable doubt

The standard of evidence required to convict someone of a crime in America.

Switchblade knife

A special kind of pocket knife with a blade contained in the handle which opens automatically by a spring when a button, lever, or switch on the handle is activated.

Trial

The public forum in which a case is tried before a judge and jury.

Unanimous

All members in agreement.

Verdict

The decision of guilt or innocence issued by a jury after a trial.

Short Summary

The play is set in a New York City Court of Law jury room in 1957. The play opens to the empty jury room, and the Judge's voice is heard, giving a set of final instructions to the jurors. We learn that this is a murder case and that, if found guilty, the mandatory sentence for the accused is the death penalty. After these instructions, the jurors enter.

The men file in and decide to take a short break before deliberating. They complain that the room is hot and without air-conditioning; even the fan doesn't work. All the jurors presume the obvious guilt of the defendant, whom we learn has been accused of killing his father. Eventually, the twelve sit down and a vote is taken. All of the jurors vote "guilty," except for the 8th Juror, who votes "not guilty," which, due to the requirement of a unanimous jury, forces them to discuss the case.

The jurors react violently against this dissenting vote. Ultimately, they decide to go around the table, explaining why they believe the boy to be guilty, in hopes of convincing 8th Juror.

Through this discussion we learn the following facts about the case: an old man living beneath the boy and his father testified that he heard upstairs a fight, the boy shouting, "I'm gonna kill you," a body hitting the ground, and then he saw the boy running down the stairs. The boy claimed he had been at the movies while his father was murdered, but couldn't remember the name of the movies or who was in them. A woman living across the street testified that she saw the boy kill his father through the windows of a passing elevated train. The boy had, that night, had an argument with his father, which resulted in the boy's father hitting him twice. Finally, the boy has an extensive list of prior offenses, including trying to slash another teenager with a knife.

There is a strong rallying against the defendant. 3rd Juror compares him to his own son, with whom he was estranged, and 10th Juror reveals strong racist tendencies against the defendant.

When a discussion about the murder weapon, which was identified as the knife purchased by the defendant, a "one-of-a-kind" knife, begins, 8th Juror surprises the others by presenting an identical knife he had purchased in a pawn shop two blocks from where the boy lived a few nights prior, shattering the claim that the knife was so unique and identifiable.

8th Juror makes a proposition that the other eleven of them could vote, and if all of them voted "not guilty," he would not stand alone and would go along with their guilty verdict. They agree to this and vote by secret ballot. The vote is 10 "guilty" votes and 1 "not guilty" vote, and so the deliberation continues.

Immediately, the jurors turn on 5th Juror, accusing him of having changed his vote out of sympathy for the boy. 9th Juror stands and admits to having changed his vote because he'd like to hear the arguments out.

8th Juror calls into question the validity of the testimony of the old man living downstairs. 9th Juror provides the possibility that the old man was only testifying to feel important. 8th Juror concludes by saying that even if he did hear him say, "I'm gonna kill you," that very well could be taken out of context as just a figure of speech. With this 5th Juror changes his vote to "not guilty," and the vote is 9-3 in favor of guilty.

After another heated discussion which raises the question of why the boy would have returned home, after killing his father, they take another vote. This time, 5th, 8th, 9th, and 11th vote "not guilty," and the deliberation continues.

After a brief argument, 8th Juror brings into question whether or not the downstairs neighbor, an old man who had suffered a stroke and could only walk slowly, could have gotten to the door to see the boy run down the stairs in fifteen seconds, as he had testified. 8th Juror recreates the floor plan of the apartment, while 2nd Juror times him, and they conclude that he would not have been able to reach his door in fifteen seconds.

3rd Juror reacts violently to this and ends up attacking 8th Juror, shouting, "God damn it! I'll kill him! I'll kill him." 8th Juror asks, "You don't really mean you'll kill me, do you?" proving his earlier point about how people say, "I'll kill you," when they don't really mean it.

Act II resumes in the same moment we left off with in Act I. After everything calms down, the jurors resume deliberations. Another vote is taken, and the jury is now six to six. They take a break. During this break, it begins to rain outside. Also, they are able to turn the fan on, cooling off the room.

When deliberations resume, 8th Juror attempts to break apart the testimony of the arresting police officer that the defendant was unable to name the movies that he had claimed to have seen that evening. He asserts that possibly the defendant just forgot the names of the films and who was in them "under great emotional distress."

Upon further discussion about the switchblade, it becomes questionable whether or not the defendant would have made the stab wound, "down and in," which would be contrary to his knowledge and experience with how to use such a knife.

The jurors take another vote, and it is now nine to three, all but 3rd, 4th, and 10th Juror are in favor of 'not guilty.' This launches 10th Juror in a massive bigoted rant, which ends with 4th Juror scolding him back into his seat.

9th Juror calls into question the eyewitness testimony of the woman living across the street, as she wore glasses but chose not to wear them in court, calling into question whether or not she would have been wearing them in bed, when she saw the murder through her window.

Now, the vote is 11 to 1, and 3rd Juror stands alone. At first, he stands firm, saying that he will be the holdout to make this a hung jury. He launches himself into a final massive rant against the boy that descends into nonsense. 8th and 4th Jurors make a short final plea, and 3rd Juror finally concedes, saying "All right. Not guilty." The Foreman informs the Guard that they have reached a verdict, and the Jurors leave the courtroom.

Quotes and Analysis

JUDGE'S VOICE: ...and that concludes the court's explanation of the legal aspects of this case. And now, gentlemen of the jury, I come to my final instruction to you. Murder in the first degree - premeditated homicide - is the most serious charge tried in our criminal courts. You've listened to the testimony and you've had the law read to you and interpreted as it applies to this case. It now becomes your duty to try and separate the facts from the fancy. One man is dead. The life of another is at stake. I urge you to deliberate honestly and thoughtfully. If this is a reasonable doubt - then you must bring me a verdict of "not guilty." If, however, there is no reasonable doubt - then you must, in good conscience, find the accused guilty. However you decide, your verdict must be unanimous. In the event you find the accused guilty, the bench will not entertain a recommendation for mercy. The death sentence is mandatory in this case. I don't envy your job. You are faced with a grave responsibility. Thank you, gentlemen.

6

This opening monologue brings us into the play. It serves two direct purposes. First, it serves as the introduction to the action of the play. We learn that the given situation is that a group of jurors must determine the guilt or innocence of this man, and we learn such specifics as that they must return a unanimous verdict and that the death sentence is mandatory, if convicted. In this sense, it is a very efficient and economical way to introduce the play.

It is also to be considered the way that Rose chooses to introduce this monologue. There is not a prequel scene where the men are addressed by the Judge, nor are the men on stage when the Judge's offstage monologue is said. Rather, it is to an empty stage, giving the effect that the monologue is not as much for the Jurors as it is for the audience themselves. It introduces a secondary dialogue in the play, in which the audience plays juror for the accused and for the Jurors on stage.

12TH JUROR: (to 8th Juror) What d'you think of the case? It had a lot of interest for me. No dead spots - know what I mean? I'll tell you we were lucky to get a murder case. I figured us for a burglary or an assault or something. Those can be the dullest.

8

This quote perfectly shows everything that Reginald Rose thinks is wrong with the American public and the justice system. Here we have someone who is about to make a decision that will either save a boy's life or kill him, and he's *happy* that it's a murder case, where a man died, because it's exciting for him. It shows a complete lack of concern, which concern 8th Juror will slowly come to impress upon the other jurors. It makes the whole event sound more like a Roman circus than an American court of law.

8TH JUROR: ...Look, this boy's been kicked around all his life. You know - living in a slum, his mother dead since he was nine. He spent a year and a half in an orphanage while his father served a jail term for forgery. That's not a very good head start. He had a pretty terrible sixteen years. I think maybe we owe him a few words. That's all.

13

In contrast to the previous monologue, this displays why 8th Juror is repeatedly characterized as the passionate, responsible model of an American citizen. He is not unreasonably confident that the boy is innocent. He admits that he is not sure, but he feels that it is the boy's right that they at least give him a fair shot. He recognizes that this boy has had hard times, and he sticks up for him. Rose represents this moment as one good American standing up for the weaker man.

3RD JUROR: Yeah, well I've got (a kid). He's twenty. We did everything for that boy, and what happened? When he was nine he ran away from a fight. I saw him. I was so ashamed I almost threw up. So I told him right out. "I'm gonna make a man outa your or I'm gonna bust you in half trying." Well, I made a man outa him all right. When he was sixteen we had a battle. He hit me in the face. He's big, y'know. I haven't seen him in two years. Rotten kid. You work your heart out...[He breaks off. He has said more than he intended. He is embarrassed.] All right. Let's get on with it.

18

Here, Rose gives us a glimpse into the irrationalities and prejudices that can play into any given member of a jury. Here, 3rd Juror reveals that he has a troubled relationship with his son, which resulted in his being in a fight, parallel to how the accused allegedly got into a fight with his father, which resulted in his death. We begin to understand that all of the members of the jury are human with an infinite number of life experiences upon which any decision might be based. They are not creatures of pure logic and reason, but people with feelings and histories.

8TH JUROR: No. I'm saying it's possible that the boy lost the knife and that someone else stabbed his father with a similar knife. It's possible.

...

[The 8th Juror stands for a moment in silence, then he reaches into his pocket and swiftly withdraws a knife. He holds it in front of his face and flicks open the blade, then he leans forward and sticks the knife into the table alongside the other. They are exactly alike. There is a burst of sound in the room.]

23

This is the first moment when 8th Juror really makes a crack into the case of the prosecutor. He proves that the knife claimed to be "one-of-a-kind" that the defendant owned wasn't as original as they may have been led to believe. Negating the legitimacy of evidence in this way lends itself to the creation of reasonable doubt, which, if it is exist, is grounds for a verdict of 'not guilty.'

6TH JUROR: I'm not used to supposing. I'm just a working man. My boss does the supposing. But I'll try one. Suppose you talk us all outa this and the kid really did knife his father?

30

This is an interesting contrast to the rest of the counterarguments we've been seeing. Previously, 8th Juror seems to be the voice of reason, and everyone else has some kind of block, preventing them from being rational. Here, 6th Juror provides a completely rational and very real argument why 8th Juror should not necessarily be so eager to acquit him. What's interesting is that the possibility remains throughout the entirety of the play that the accused really did kill his father. Naturally, we come to be on the side of the hero, 8th Juror, and naturally root for a verdict of 'not guilty,' but we cannot ever shake the reality that there's a very real chance that the accused did, in fact, murder his father, in which case justice would not have been served.

9TH JUROR: It's just that I looked at him for a very long time. The seam of his jacket was split under his arm. Did you notice it? I mean, to come to court like that. He was a very old man with a torn jacket and he walked very slowly to the stand. He was dragging his left leg and trying to hide it because he was ashamed. I think I know him better than anyone here. This is a quiet, frightened, insignificant old man who has been nothing all his life, who has never had recognition, his name in the newspapers. Nobody knows him, nobody quotes him, nobody seeks his advice after seventy-five years. That's a very sad thing, to be nothing. A man like this needs to be recognized, to be listened to, to be quoted just once. This is very important. It would be so hard for him to recede into the background...

36

This marks a shift in the tactic of argument. Previously, we have seen 8th Juror try, piece by piece, to challenge the validity of the evidence. However, here 9th Juror considers a much more humanistic approach of considering the evidence. He ponders the old man and extrapolates a completely synthesized understanding of this old man. It is very compelling and affects some of the other jurors. The difference between this argument and the others previously given is that this one has nothing to do with any of the evidence. 9th Juror doesn't actually know anything about this old man. For all he knows, his jacket ripped on the door as he was walking into the building, but he takes these context clues to explain and discredit the old man's testimony. We are moved, as an audience. However, we cannot help but acknowledge the fact that it might be complete garbage.

8TH JUROR: But supposing he really did hear it. This phrase, how many times has each of us used it? Probably hundreds, "I could kill you for doing that, darling." "If you do that once more, Junior, I'm going to kill you." "Come on, Rocky, kill him." We say it every day. It doesn't mean we're going to kill someone.

3RD JUROR: Shut up, you son of a bitch! Let me go, God damn it! I'll kill him! I'll kill him!

8TH JUROR: You don't really mean you'll kill me, do you?

37 / 48

These two complimentary moments mark a turning point in the argument. The conflict between 3rd Juror and 8th Juror reaches a boiling point, and 3rd Juror attacks him. However, what he inadvertently does is prove an earlier point of 8th Juror. This further serves to intensify the conflict between the two, further casting them by Rose as the protagonist and antagonist, which conflict continues to be a massive obstacle for 8th Juror.

Furthermore, what it does for the audience and for the other jurors is to completely ruin the credibility of 3rd Juror as an impartial observer and juror. 8th Juror has managed to make 3rd Juror look like a mad man to the other jurors, and he becomes increasingly less effective in his efforts to maintain support throughout the second act.

11TH JUROR: ...If you want to vote not guilty, then do it because you're convinced the man is not guilty - not because you've had enough. And if you think he's guilty, then vote that way, or don't you have the guts to do what you think is right?

Quotes and Analysis

11th Juror here says one of the most important maxims of the play. Reginald Rose surely doesn't ask society to acquit every defendant, or even to acquit just the poor ones. The play asks that if you are brought into a jury room, you respect the process and treat it and those at stake with the dignity deserved. On a broader level, the play asks you to simply do what you think is right. In this moment, 7th Juror has changed his vote to 'not guilty' because he's tired of arguing, and he sees the tide of opinion swaying in that direction. 11th Juror admonishes him for this, despite the fact that he, himself, was on the 'not guilty' side. More than he wants the boy acquitted, he wants the group of jurors to do what is right, and that means following your honest, unbiased opinion, whatever that may be.

3RD JUROR: ...That goddamn rotten kid. I know him. What they're like. What they do to you. How they kill you every day. My God, don't you see? How come I'm the only one who sees? Jeez, I can feel that knife goin' in.

8TH JUROR: It's not your boy. He's somebody else.

4TH JUROR: Let him live.

[There's a long pause.]

3RD JUROR: All right. "Not guilty."

72

This is the climax of the play. When once it was 8th Juror versus 11, it is now 3rd Juror versus 11. He makes a passionate plea to convict the boy, which slowly descends into a rant which makes it very clear that he is unable to separate his feelings for his own son and the defendant. This becomes increasingly apparent over the course of the speech. 8th and 4th plead that he see that his views are not based in rationality, and he still has the choice to do what is right. Interestingly, Rose allows for this moment to be a kind of victory for everyone. It is a victory for the defendant, who is now acquitted, and who we now believe to be (possibly!) innocent. It is a victory for the audience, who has come to support 8th Juror and the defendant. It is a victory for 8th Juror, in his crusade of justice, but it is also a victory for 3rd Juror, who is finally able to face his own prejudices and his own internal conflict regarding his son and ultimately choose to do the right thing and vote 'not guilty.' He is not defeated as much as he finally defeats his own inner demons.

Summary and Analysis of Act One (Part 1)

The play is set in a New York City Court of Law jury room in 1957. The play opens to the empty jury room, and the Judge's voice is heard, giving a set of final instructions to the jurors. We learn that this is a murder case and that, if found guilty, the mandatory sentence for the accused is the death penalty. After these instructions, the jurors enter. These are 2nd-12th Juror and the Foreman.

The men file in and decide to take a short break before deliberating. They talk casually and we begin to meet some of the jurors. They complain that the room is hot and without air-conditioning; even the fan doesn't work. All who talk about the case seem flippant about the situation, and all presume the obvious guilt of the defendant, who we learn has been accused of killing his father. Eventually, the twelve sit down and a vote is taken. All of the jurors vote "guilty," except for the 8th Juror, who votes "not guilty," which, due to the requirement of a unanimous jury, forces them to discuss the case.

The other jurors react aggressively to his dissenting vote, trying to quickly talk him out of it, but 8th Juror remains convinced that he is "not sure" whether or not the boy is guilty and feels that they owe it to him to talk about the case for at least an hour, just to make sure. He cites the boy's troubled upbringing, with his mother dead and his father jailed. Jurors try to argue with him, most notably 10th Juror, who makes a particularly racist argument against the defendant, saying that "they're born liars." 12th Juror isn't even paying attention, doodling an ad idea for his marketing campaign.

Ultimately, they decide to go around the table, explaining why they believe the boy to be guilty, in hopes of convincing 8th Juror.

Through this discussion we learn the following facts about the case: an old man living beneath the boy and his father testified that he heard upstairs a fight, the boy shouting, "I'm gonna kill you," a body hitting the ground, and then he saw the boy running down the stairs. The boy claimed he had been at the movies while his father was murdered, but couldn't remember the name of the movies or who was in them. A woman living across the street testified that she saw the boy kill his father through the windows of a passing elevated train. The boy had, that night, had an argument with his father, which resulted in the boy's father hitting him twice. Finally, the boy has an extensive list of prior offenses, including trying to slash another teenager with a knife.

3rd Juror makes a speech about how this boy is just another example of "how kids are nowadays." He speaks about his own son, with whom he had a rough relationship, and to whom he hasn't spoken in two years, after a fight in which his son hit him. 10th Juror and 5th Juror get into an argument over 10th Juror's citing the boy's slum background as evidence for his being "trash." 5th Juror is angered by this, having grown up in a slum himself.

8th Juror is now made to stand and defend his "not guilty" vote for the boy. He states that he's not sure whether or not the boy did it, but he was unsatisfied with the job of the defense council, and he was unsure of the two eyewitnesses. This leads into a discussion about the knife. 4th Juror explains that, on the night of the murder, the boy bought a uniquely carved switchblade knife identical to the one used in the murder. The boy claims that he lost it that night, before coming home to find his father dead. 4th Juror presents the death weapon, the "only one of its kind;" 8th Juror surprises the others by presenting an identical knife he had purchased in a pawn shop two blocks from where the boy lived a few nights prior, shattering the claim that the knife was unique and identifiable. An argument breaks out among the jurors as to the new doubt; most are just upset that they're still arguing and want to just declare him guilty and go home.

8th Juror makes a proposition that the other eleven of them could vote, and if all of them voted "not guilty," he would not stand alone and would go along with their guilty verdict. They agree to this and vote by secret ballot. The vote is 10 "guilty" votes and 1 "not guilty" vote, and so the deliberation continues.

--- Analysis of Act One (Part 1) ---

Twelve Angry Men is in many ways a love letter to the American legal justice system. We find here eleven men, swayed to conclusions by prejudices, past experience, and short-sightedness, challenged by one man who holds himself and his peers to a higher standard of justice, demanding that this marginalized member of society be given his due process. We see the jurors struggle between the two, seemingly conflicting, purposes of a jury, to punish the guilty and to protect the innocent. It proves, however, that the logic of the American trial-by-jury system does work.

On another level, the play is about America and its makeup as a melting pot of different cultures, ideas, beliefs, and temperaments. This jury runs the gamut from a German immigrant watchmaker, 11th Juror, to a presumably wealthy broker, 4th Juror, to a male nurse at a Harlem hospital, who grew up in the slums, 5th Juror. These men represent the incredible richness of diversity in America and the various challenges that it presents. This clash becomes a major part of the conflict within the play; Rose externalizes this conflict by making the room hot, which both represents and adds to their hot temperament. Just as much as these men are trying to come up with a verdict, they are figuring out how to work together and cooperate toward a common goal. At first, this seems nearly impossible, but they slowly are able to work together.

Throughout the play, we see a variety of rhetorical strategies, used by all of the jury members to relay their belief. 8th juror appeals to their sense of pathos and pity by saying "this boy's been kicked around all his life...He's had a pretty terrible sixteen years. I think maybe we owe him a few words. That's all." While this has nothing to do with the case, he hopes to appeal to their humanity in order to get them to give him a chance in these deliberations. Many of the jurors use logos, logic and reasoning, to lay out the evidence in a rational and concrete manner to convince him. An example is when 4th Juror lays out all of the evidence of the knife to convince 8th Juror with seven, linear, factual points. The reader and audience is meant to connect a sense of ethos, reliability or competence, to 8th Juror, as he is the only one who doesn't, at first, seem to be clouded by ignorance, racism, disinterest, or any other characteristic that might cloud judgment.

The play is very interesting in its structure because we see none of the trial or events leading up to the trial. At its opening, we simply get a set of jury instructions from the judge, as if we the reader and audience are the ones about to make a judgment. We learn the facts of the case in piecemeal from the jury members, as they discuss the evidence. While the surface of the play is clearly about the trial and coming to a verdict, eliminating these outside dramatic influences shifts the focus to the jurors themselves and their own process of discovery. The play becomes just as much about their learning to deal with each other and understand themselves as it is about their coming to a verdict.

Furthermore, the play provides us with almost no specifics. At no point in the script are any names used, including for the jurors, the defendants, or the witnesses. This is a very conspicuous choice that allows each character to function as part of this larger allegory for the American society. It gives the sense that the jurors could be you, the person sitting next to you, or the person down the street; these are everyday Americans. While the setting is marked in the stage directions for the 2004 production as New York City, 1957 (which is notably the date and setting of the classic Sidney Lumet film adaptation), there are almost no factors of this play that truly force it in that setting, except perhaps that all of the jurors are men, and such tiny details as the fact that the defendant claimed to have gone to a "double feature" movie, which one would no longer find at a movie theater.

Summary and Analysis of Act One (Part 2)

--- Summary of Act One (Part 2) ---

Immediately, the jurors turn on 5th Juror, accusing him of having changed his vote out of sympathy for the boy. 9th Juror stands and admits to having changed his vote because he'd like to hear the arguments out. The men take a break. We learn that the 11th juror is a German watchmaker. 12th Juror works for an advertisement agency. 8th Juror is an architect, and 7th Juror sells marmalade.

8th Juror presents several hypothetical situations, based on the father's criminal background, that could have gotten him killed that evening. Next, he attempts to discount the testimony by the old man living downstairs by deducing that, because of the sound made by the elevated train passing by, there's no way he could have heard with certainty screaming and a body hitting the floor. 9th Juror identifies with the poor old man, believing that he might just be trying to feel important. 8th Juror concludes by saying that even if he did hear him say, "I'm gonna kill you," that very well could be taken out of context as just a figure of speech. With this 5th Juror changes his vote to "not guilty," and the vote is 9-3 in favor of guilty.

11th Juror raises another question of why the boy would return home, several hours after his father had been murdered, if he had been the one to murder him. 4th Juror suggests that he left the knife in a state of panic and then decided to come back for it later, but 11th Juror challenges this by reminding him that the fingerprints had been wiped off the knife, suggesting that the murderer left calmly. There is more question over the accuracy of the witnesses, and an argument breaks out. 8th Juror calls for another vote. This time, 5th, 8th, 9th, and 11th vote "not guilty," and the deliberation continues.

After a brief argument, 8th Juror brings into question whether or not the downstairs neighbor, an old man who had suffered a stroke and could only walk slowly, could have gotten to the door to see the boy run down the stairs in fifteen seconds, as he had testified. 8th Juror recreates the floor plan of the apartment, while 2nd Juror times him, and they conclude that he would not have been able to reach his door in fifteen seconds.

3rd Juror reacts violently to this, calling it dishonest, saying that this kid had "got to burn." 8th Juror calls him a "self-appointed public avenger" and a "sadist," and 3rd leaps at him. Restrained by the other men, he shouts, "God damn it! I'll kill him! I'll kill him." 8th Juror asks, "You don't really mean you'll kill me, do you?" proving his earlier point about how people say, "I'll kill you," when they don't really mean it.

--- Analysis of Act One (Part 2) ---

In this section, the play begins to divide its jurors into three categories. First, 8th Juror stands alone as fighting for the boy. Now, one may include 9th Juror in this, as he does quickly become an advocate for the boy, after hearing a few of 8th Juror's arguments. Second, there are jurors who do presume the defendant to be guilty, but aren't belligerent about their beliefs, simply convinced that he is guilty. This would include 2nd, 4th, 5th, 6th, 11th, and 12th Jurors. 3rd, 7th, and 10th Jurors seem particularly prejudiced or indifferent against the boy and are unmoved by the arguments of the others in this first act. For them, it is greater than simply changing their mind about the case; it requires them to challenge notions held deep within themselves.

8th Juror is clearly set up by Rose as the protagonist. He is characterized as level-headed and fair. At the beginning of the play, he is contemplating the case seriously, with due consideration, as opposed to many of the other jurors who treat it frivolously or don't seem to care much at all. When the vote is taken, he votes "not guilty," not because he is certain of the boy's innocence, which would be a hard sell by any account, but he simply says, "I don't know." He wants to talk through the case and see what conclusion they find, as opposed to jumping to a guilty verdict. We are clearly meant to view him as doing the right, though difficult, thing. He is a classic hero, faced by what seems to be an overwhelming challenge, to convince these men. In this first act, we see him remain stoic and steadfast in his quest for justice, in the face of much opposition and nastiness, embodying an American ideal.

Furthermore, the scope of the play expands to become about how people come to decisions. The individual psychologies of the jury members interact in a very complex manner. Earlier in the act, it seemed very clear that it is a group of men against 8th Juror, and that group seemed to speak with one voice, using the same logic. However, as the play progresses, we see that each of the jurors came to their decision in a very different manner. 2nd Juror seems to have been swayed simply by the tone of the courtroom, which is reflective of his characterization as meek, perhaps susceptible to popular influence. We are encouraged to believe that 3rd Juror's opinion is influenced by his bad relationship with his son, and 4th Juror seems to be completely reliant upon the facts of the case. Here, the group psychology breaks down into the individual psychology. Where this group of eleven found it so easy to convict him jointly, it becomes harder for them, as their individual beliefs and motivations are put on trial.

Summary and Analysis of Act Two

Act II resumes in the same moment we left Act I. 3rd Juror has just, in a fury, tried to leap at 8th Juror, but is restrained. The Guard enters, and everything calms down; the jurors resume deliberations. Another vote is taken, and the jury is now six to six. They take a break. During this break, it begins to rain outside. Also, they are able to turn the fan on, cooling the room. 3rd Juror tries to reclaim some of his image; he talks to 4th juror, saying, "I get moved by this. But let me tell you, I'm sincere." 4th Juror does not respond well, indicating that 3rd Juror has, in fact, lost credibility.

When deliberations resume, 8th Juror attempts to break apart the testimony of the arresting police officer that the defendant was unable to name the movies that he had claimed to have seen that evening. He asserts that possibly the defendant just forgot the names of the films and who was in them "under great emotional distress." He illustrates this point by asking 4th Juror what he saw several nights ago at the movies. 4th Juror is unable to respond accurately, and the point is made.

The Foreman brings up the fact that a psychologist testified that after giving the defendant several tests, he determined that the defendant had homicidal tendencies. However, 11th Juror argues against this piece of evidence reminding the jurors that there is a big difference between having homicidal tendencies and committing murder.

Next, 2nd Juror brings up the coroner's testimony that the father had been stabbed in the chest "down and in" and also that his father was six or seven inches taller than he. While reenacting the mechanics of this stabbing, 5th Juror gets up and begins to examine the switchblade. He explains that it would make no sense for someone to stab someone like that with a switchblade because it would require the attacker to lose precious time. Because the defendant was highly competent with a switchblade, it becomes questionable whether or not he would have made that chest wound.

7th Juror, tired of sitting through these deliberations, decides to change his vote to 'not guilty.' 11th Juror is angered by this, furious that 7th Juror is not respecting the process enough to do what he believes is right, no matter what that is. The jurors take another vote, and it is now nine to three, all but 3rd, 4th, and 10th Juror are in favor of 'not guilty.' This launches 10th Juror in a massive bigoted rant, which ends with 4th Juror scolding him back into his seat.

4th Juror now begins a discussion by reintroducing what he considers to be the most compelling piece of evidence, the testimony of the woman across the street, who claims to have heard a scream and then to have seen him stab his father through the windows of the elevated train passing by. While he is speaking, he rubs his nose where his spectacles have made indentations. This causes 9th Juror to realize that the woman also had those same marks on her nose and must have worn glasses, despite the fact that she didn't wear them in court, presumably for her own vanity. This causes all of the jurors to question the eyesight of the woman, who may have witnessed the murder without her glasses. Based on this, 4th Juror changes his vote. 10th Juror gives up and also changes his vote to "not guilty."

Now, the vote is 11 to 1, and 3rd Juror stands alone. At first, he stands firm, saying that he will be the holdout to make this a hung jury. He launches himself into a final massive rant against the boy that descends into nonsense. 8th and 4th Jurors make a short final plea, and 3rd Juror finally concedes, saying "All right. Not guilty." The Foreman informs the Guard that they have reached a verdict, and the Jurors leave the courtroom.

--- Analysis of Act Two ---

Act II operates in many ways as a reversal of Act I. We see the characters reduced down to their most basic composition, based on how they process the evidence. Besides being a halfway point in the case, it marks a halfway mark in 8th Juror's campaign to convince the other jurors of the defendant's innocence, with a 6-6 vote taken early in the first act. Whereas in Act I, it seems like the impossible task, now they are on even footing, and the momentum is certainly on his side.

It's very interesting that Reginald Rose does not provide us in this second act with any massive realization that would prove the innocence of the defendant. In fact, it seems that the arguments for his innocence become weaker and weaker. 8th Juror uses 4th Juror's failure to remember the names and stars of a movie to prove that it's very easy to forget such details under great emotional stress, but meanwhile 4th Juror was able to name one of the films and comes close to being able to name the second film, in addition to who starred in it. It would seem that 4th Juror has passed 8th Juror's test, but 8th Juror is able to frame it in such a way that makes him seem correct. While clearly framing 8th Juror as the hero of the play, Rose is very conscious not to make him overwhelmingly right, to maintain a sense of doubt.

10th and 3rd Juror, the two last remaining holdouts for a guilty verdict, are brought to light in this second act. In Act I, we saw both being guided by their prejudices, but what seemed to be a gentle nod in Act I toward the subconscious psychologies of jurors comes into full view in Act II, when both are given long monologues that fully outline the prejudices that govern their decisions. 10th Juror says, "They're against us, they hate us, they want to destroy us…There's a danger." This is a fascinating choice because he's speaking about the danger of the defendant, but everyone in the room – and in the audience – realizes that 10th Juror is the actual danger. He is the one that is polluting our society and is a danger to our legal system and way of life. It's a dangerous discovery, as it blatantly dramatizes the incredibly strong prejudices that can lay hidden in the American subconscious.

Similarly, we see that 3rd Juror, who has, despite his temper, been a somewhat coherent voice in the deliberations, is completely driven by his own demons to convict the boy, in place of his own son, with whom he has a troubled relationship. We see the layers of his decision making process peel away in his final monologue. It begins with him chronicling logically the case; however, it quickly becomes clear that he is no longer talking about the defendant. He says, "I can feel the knife goin' in," and we see that his personal connection and confusion about the case runs deep. Finally, the demon is named when 8th Juror says, "It's not your boy. It's somebody else." 3rd Juror finally gives in to reason. The play seems to be telling us that if we recognize and name our prejudices, we are able to defeat them, and ultimately do what is right.

The theme of heat becomes apparent in this act, as the oppressive heat of Act I is cooled by the rains and the discovery of a fan in the room. It seems that as the temperature of the room decreases, so does the temperament of the jurors, and they are able to operate more rationally.

The very ending of the play, which just has the jurors walking out, shows that the play was not about the verdict and the defendant. If it were, the final scene would be the judge reading a "not guilty" verdict. However, the climax is rather 3rd Juror facing his internal conflict and winning against it. The play is about a group of men just trying to do what is right, and they ultimately succeed.

Suggested Essay Questions

1. **How does Rose maintain doubt as to the defendant's guilt or innocence throughout the play?**

   Rose accomplishes this factual ambiguity by never actually allowing any of the jurors to definitively prove his innocence. Instead, they are only really able to prove that he is not definitely guilty, or "not guilty beyond a reasonable doubt." There are many reasonable arguments as to why he may very well have been guilty, but they ultimately don't prove strong enough to convict.

2. **Explain how the idea of 'reasonable doubt' particularly pertains to this case.**

   In the American criminal system, those charged with crimes need to be proven guilty 'beyond a reasonable doubt.' It is up to a jury to decide what that means and how to apply it in the case. Here, 8th Juror was able to put enough doubt into their minds, by challenging the evidence, to prove to them that they could not be sure enough to convict the defendant.

3. **Give examples of how the personal insight of the jurors affected their understanding of the case?**

   9th Juror is able to offer up to the other jurors a particular reading of the old man who testified, as he felt like he "knew" him, perhaps based on a shared life experience. This affected the way he understood his testimony. More concretely, 5th Juror grew up around knife fights, where switchblades were commonly used, which allowed him to offer insight into how a wound would or would not be made.

4. **What examples of prejudice can be found in the play?**

   10th Juror is the most obvious example, immediately against the defendant just because he was "one of them." Similarly, 3rd Juror is prejudiced against the defendant because he reminds him of his own son, from whom he is estranged. On the other extreme, 8th Juror is prejudiced to give the defendant special consideration because he had a hard upbringing and comes from a poor background.

5. **What role does the Foreman play in controlling the other jurors?**

   On a practical level, the Foreman is charged with moderating their discussion and taking regular polls as to the judgment of the jurors. In this instance, he has the much grander job of controlling the many larger and temperamental personalities in the room. He is criticized at points for how he controls the room, but ultimately is able to keep the room from descending into chaos. In some ways, he represents the American self-governance system.

6. **Why might Rose have decided to place the division of Acts I and II where he did?**

On a dramatic level, Act I ends with a very exciting moment that would serve to make a powerful end to the first act, right before an intermission. Also, it marks a very important moment in the play where the balance of power shifts. 3rd Juror loses control, leaping at 8th Juror, proving one of 8th Juror's point and making himself look unstable and unreliable. Act II is also marked by a different tone, outwardly manifested by the changing weather.

7. **How do the conditions of the jury room mimic the attitudes of the jurors?**

One of the first thing the jurors comment on is the temperature in the room, which is oppressively hot. It seems that Rose uses this as a device to emphasize the heated discussions going on inside the room. Also, we might think that these men are driven to madness quickly by the heat. In the second act, it begins raining outside, and they are able to turn on the fan, marking a return to reason for many of the jurors.

8. **How is 8th Juror represented as the hero of the play?**

While we are unsure whether he is right or wrong, 8th Juror is one of the only jurors who is unaffected by any kind of negative prejudices. He respects the system and the value of life, causing him to want to consider the case more carefully than others. He is motivated simply by the idea of surviving justice and no other personal gain or affirmation comes into play.

9. **Compare and contrast the rational and irrational arguments for guilt from the jurors.**

4th Juror is able to move through the evidence logically and thoroughly, determining that the defendant is most certainly guilty. Similarly, 6th Juror is moved away from the idea that they can't have any doubt and convict him, based on the very real fear of putting a killer back on the streets. Conversely, we have 10th Juror, who irrationally presumes guilt upon the defendant because of his ethnicity and background. The difference is that the former arguments are founded in evidence and logic, while the latter is not.

10. **How does the fact that the jurors are all male impact the play?**

Rose definitely plays off of the masculine energy to create these archetypical characters. The title of the play is '12 Angry Men,' and it certainly does have an understanding of how particularly men settle problems in a confrontational, often personal, manner. There is a definite competitiveness, especially between 3rd Juror and 8th Juror, that is somehow intrinsically masculine. The idea of the father/son relationship is so strong because we have the understanding of each one of these men as a potential father, some confirmed.

Naturalism and the American Style

This play is both characteristic of the American style of the time and also fairly unique. An understanding of the style of theater from which this play emerged allows us to have a very interesting look into it.

This play would be considered naturalistic, taking place over one continuous span of time and in one place. Furthermore, it features language that is natural-style prose (it sounds like how normal people speak). The goal of this is not just to show how people are but also why they are the way that they are. For example, we find out that 3rd Juror is impacted by the experience of having a son. Physical factors are taken into account as well, such as the temperature of the room. All of these are taken into direct consideration and impact the story.

The prevailing American style at the time was realism, which is much like naturalism, except that it is much more apt to deal with time disjointedly. However, it is very important to note that the first incarnation of this full play was, in fact, as a play for television. Although we are now accustomed to television programs using many locations and scenes like movies do, at the time it was far more common for teleplays and episodic dramas to take place on single sets, like a stage play. Therefore, the teleplay takes advantage of the limitations of its format to enhance themes and present a narrative that *should* take place in just one room.

On one hand, courtroom drama "who-dun-its" are certainly a favorite form of storytelling for American audiences. However, this play turns that on its head by not showing those involved or even investigating the case, but those who are sequestered to review the case, the jurors. This is a fairly abnormal choice, but what it does is change the focus of the play. We are no longer watching a play about figuring out whether or not the defendant killed his father, a fairly simple model, but rather we are trying to figure out how these men will learn to work with one another and whether or not they'll be able to overcome themselves and do what is right.

Naturalism and the American Style

Author of ClassicNote and Sources

Sean Peter Drohan, author of ClassicNote. Completed on February 25, 2012, copyright held by GradeSaver.

Updated and revised Elizabeth Weinbloom April 30, 2012. Copyright held by GradeSaver.

Readings on Twelve Angry Men. Baumbach, Jonathan. San Diego, CA: Greenhaven, 2000.

Kevin Dowler. "Reginald Rose." 2012-02-17. <http://www.museum.tv/eotvsection.php?entrycode=rosereginal>.

Jost, Walter. "Sweating The Little Things In Sidney Lumet's 12 Angry Men." The Ethos of Rhetoric. 75-88. Columbia, SC: U of South Carolina P, 2004. MLA International Bibliography. Web. 17 Feb. 2012.

Quiz 1

1. **By what kind of knife is the victim stabbed?**
   A. Butcher knife
   B. Butterfly knife
   C. Steak knife
   D. Switchblade knife

2. **What was unique about the knife used to stab the victim?**
   A. The metal in the blade
   B. A strangely long blade
   C. Its ivory accent
   D. The carving on its handle

3. **What does the defendant claim he was doing while his father was stabbed?**
   A. Bowling
   B. Riding his bike
   C. Going to the movies
   D. Getting into a fight

4. **Which juror votes 'not guilty' at the first vote?**
   A. 3rd
   B. 5th
   C. 8th
   D. 10th

5. **Which is the last juror to vote 'not guilty?'**
   A. 2nd Juror
   B. 3rd Juror
   C. 9th Juror
   D. 11th Juror

6. **How is the stab wound described by the jurors?**
   A. Diagonal and ripping
   B. Down and in
   C. Deep and repeated
   D. Up and across

7. What was the defendant's height in relation to his father?

A. Taller

B. The play does not say.

C. Shorter

D. Exactly the same

8. According to the stage directions, when does this play take place?

A. 1950

B. 1955

C. 1956

D. 1957

9. With what crime is the defendant charged?

A. Manslaughter

B. Assault with a deadly weapon

C. 2nd Degree Murder

D. 1st Degree Murder

10. How many of the 12 jurors must vote 'guilty' for a conviction?

A. 7

B. 8

C. 11

D. 12

11. 7th Juror wants the deliberation to end so that he can get to what event?

A. A baseball game

B. A broadway show

C. His daughter's birthday party

D. A business meeting

12. 12th Juror is frequently making reference to his job as a what?

A. Doctor

B. Lawyer

C. School teacher

D. Advertising agent

13. **What was the problem with the jury room?**
    A. Too small
    B. Heat
    C. Smelled like rotten eggs
    D. Cold

14. **The woman across the street witnessed the murder through what?**
    A. Bushes
    B. A clothesline
    C. Her binoculars
    D. An elevated train

15. **Who was the first juror to join 8th Juror with a 'not guilty' vote?**
    A. 2nd Juror
    B. 4th Juror
    C. 9th Juror
    D. 10th Juror

16. **Why did the defendant claim to have purchased a knife the night of the murder?**
    A. To give it to his friend
    B. For woodcarving
    C. For protection from his father
    D. For a planned knife fight

17. **What type of business does 3rd Juror run?**
    A. Construction
    B. Plumbing
    C. Air Conditioning
    D. Messenger

18. **What did the old man living underneath the defendant testify to hearing him say?**
    A. I'll get you this time
    B. You're not gonna hurt me again
    C. I'm gonna kill you
    D. You're gonna regret this

19. **How old is the defendant?**
    A. 12
    B. 16
    C. 20
    D. 23

20. **According to the stage directions, where does this play take place?**
    A. Chicago
    B. Hollywood
    C. Pittsburgh
    D. New York City

21. **What is the woman across the street doing when she witnesses the murder?**
    A. Reading a book
    B. Watching television
    C. Knitting a scarf
    D. Lying in bed

22. **Which juror grew up in the slums?**
    A. 5th Juror
    B. 7th Juror
    C. 8th Juror
    D. 12th Juror

23. **Why did the old man walk slowly?**
    A. He had a stroke
    B. He had a prosthetic leg
    C. He was frightened
    D. Old age

24. **How did 8th Juror cast doubt on the uniqueness of the murder weapon?**
    A. By finding and producing an exact match
    B. By providing similar knives that confuse the other jurors
    C. By providing statistics about knife manufacturing
    D. By making a knife that looks much the same

25. **Why wouldn't the old man have been able to hear the defendant's voice?**

    A. The television was on

    B. The gunshot would have obscured the voice

    C. The train was passing by

    D. He is hard of hearing

Quiz 1 Answer Key

1. **(D)** Switchblade knife
2. **(D)** The carving on its handle
3. **(C)** Going to the movies
4. **(C)** 8th
5. **(B)** 3rd Juror
6. **(B)** Down and in
7. **(C)** Shorter
8. **(D)** 1957
9. **(D)** 1st Degree Murder
10. **(D)** 12
11. **(A)** A baseball game
12. **(D)** Advertising agent
13. **(B)** Heat
14. **(B)** A clothesline
15. **(C)** 9th Juror
16. **(A)** To give it to his friend
17. **(D)** Messenger
18. **(C)** I'm gonna kill you
19. **(B)** 16
20. **(D)** New York City
21. **(D)** Lying in bed
22. **(A)** 5th Juror
23. **(A)** He had a stroke
24. **(A)** By finding and producing an exact match
25. **(C)** The train was passing by

Quiz 2

1. **What did 8th Juror call 3rd Juror that provoked him to attack him?**
   A. Sadist
   B. Jerk
   C. Devil
   D. Idiot

2. **Why didn't 10th Juror like the defendant?**
   A. He didn't like the sound of his voice
   B. He thought that he was unremorseful
   C. He didn't like the way he dressed
   D. He was racist against him

3. **What does the defendant claim happened to the knife?**
   A. It was stolen from him
   B. It broke in a fight
   C. He had given it to a friend
   D. He dropped it

4. **What was 8th Juror's occupation?**
   A. Doctor
   B. Architect
   C. Therapist
   D. Professor

5. **What brings the woman's testimony into question?**
   A. Her love for the father
   B. Her hearing
   C. Her eyesight
   D. Her hatred of the boy

6. **What was the time of death of the father?**
   A. Midnight
   B. 1am
   C. 10pm
   D. 11pm

7. Where did 8th Juror find that identical knife?
A. He bought it from a kid
B. He made it
C. In a pawn shop
D. On the street

8. Who gives the jurors' instructions at the beginning of the play?
A. The Judge
B. The Guard
C. The Foreman
D. The Prosecuting Attorney

9. If convicted, what is the punishment for the defendant?
A. Life in prison
B. 20 years in prison
C. 50 years in prison
D. Death

10. How was the father killed?
A. Poison
B. Gun shot
C. Stabbing
D. Fell to his death

11. Where is the father wounded?
A. Stomach
B. Back
C. Head
D. Chest

12. Where does the old man who testified live?
A. In the basement
B. Across the street
C. Downstairs
D. Down the hall

13. **Where does the woman who testified live?**
    A. In the basement
    B. Across the hall
    C. Across the street
    D. Downstairs

14. **Why is the woman eyewitness awake?**
    A. She is an insomniac
    B. It is too hot
    C. She is working late
    D. It is too cold

15. **How were the defendant and victim related?**
    A. Father and son
    B. Mother and son
    C. Friends
    D. Brothers

16. **How many people voted guilty in the first vote?**
    A. 1
    B. 4
    C. 7
    D. 11

17. **What about the jury room improved in Act II?**
    A. They were moved to a new room
    B. The guard brought in a new fan
    C. It cooled down because of night
    D. They figured out how to turn on the fan

18. **What is the vote count at the beginning of Act II?**
    A. 7-4
    B. 6-6
    C. 11-1
    D. 8-3

19. **Through how many cars of the EL train did the witness see the murder?**
    A. 1
    B. 3
    C. 4
    D. 6

20. **What is 4th Juror's occupation?**
    A. Teacher
    B. Diplomat
    C. Accountant
    D. Stock broker

21. **What side job does the 2nd Juror have?**
    A. Shoe shiner
    B. Assistant football coach
    C. Poker player
    D. Boxer

22. **Where does 5th Juror work?**
    A. A grocery store
    B. Harlem Hospital
    C. Macy's
    D. He does not have a job

23. **What is 6th Juror's occupation**
    A. Lawyer
    B. Writer
    C. Milk Man
    D. Painter

24. **11th Juror is from where?**
    A. Mexico
    B. Russia
    C. Germany
    D. Hollywood

25. What is 11th Juror's occupation?
A. Tailor
B. Lawyer
C. Watchmaker
D. Stock broker

Quiz 2 Answer Key

1. **(A)** Sadist
2. **(D)** He was racist against him
3. **(D)** He dropped it
4. **(B)** Architect
5. **(C)** Her eyesight
6. **(A)** Midnight
7. **(C)** In a pawn shop
8. **(A)** The Judge
9. **(D)** Death
10. **(C)** Stabbing
11. **(D)** Chest
12. **(C)** Downstairs
13. **(C)** Across the street
14. **(B)** It is too hot
15. **(A)** Father and son
16. **(D)** 11
17. **(D)** They figured out how to turn on the fan
18. **(B)** 6-6
19. **(B)** 3
20. **(D)** Stock broker
21. **(B)** Assistant football coach
22. **(B)** Harlem Hospital
23. **(D)** Painter
24. **(C)** Germany
25. **(C)** Watchmaker

Quiz 3

1. **What is 12th Juror's occupation?**
    A. Doctor
    B. Used car salesman
    C. Advertising agent
    D. Real estate broker

2. **7th Juror teases the foreman by calling him what?**
    A. Willie
    B. Mr. Stingy
    C. Kid
    D. Jerk

3. **10th Juror is afflicted how?**
    A. Headache
    B. A nosebleed
    C. A cold
    D. Sharp pain in his leg

4. **12 Angry Men began as what?**
    A. A short story
    B. A novel
    C. A teleplay
    D. A true story

5. **What happens if the jurors cannot come to a unanimous decision?**
    A. They must continue discussing until they come to an agreement
    B. The defendant is declared 'not guilty'
    C. The judge makes a ruling
    D. They are a 'hung jury'

6. **What happened between the victim and defendant on the night of the murder?**
    A. They peacefully ate dinner together
    B. They had a fight, and the victim (his father) struck him
    C. They had a fight, and the defendant beat the victim (his father)
    D. They did not see each other that evening

7. **The old man testified to have gotten out of his bed to the door in how long?**
   A. 20 seconds
   B. 30 seconds
   C. 15 seconds
   D. 60 seconds

8. **What is wrong with the clothes of the old man who testified?**
   A. His shoes have a hole in them
   B. His pants don't fit
   C. His sleeve is torn
   D. His shirt had stains on it

9. **Where is Reginald Rose from?**
   A. Chicago
   B. LA
   C. Miami
   D. New York City

10. **Reginald Rose primarily wrote for what medium?**
    A. Movies
    B. Novels
    C. Television
    D. Stage

11. **Reginald Rose's writing is particularly concerned with what?**
    A. Social issues
    B. Literary form
    C. Personal psychology
    D. Love and sex

12. **In what year did 12 Angry Men receive its Broadway debut?**
    A. 1957
    B. 1964
    C. 1983
    D. 2004

13. **When was 12 Angry Men made into a movie?**
    A. 1955
    B. 1957
    C. 1964
    D. 2004

14. **Who starred as 8th Juror in the original 12 Angry Men film?**
    A. James Stewart
    B. Humphrey Bogart
    C. Henry Fonda
    D. Paul Newman

15. **Who starred as 8th Juror in the 1997 tv remake?**
    A. Sir. Lawrence Olivier
    B. Jack Lemmon
    C. Sir. Anthony Hopkins
    D. George C. Scott

16. **What style does this play best represent?**
    A. Realism
    B. Post-Modernism
    C. Naturalism
    D. Surrealism

17. **What happens to the weather at the beginning of Act II?**
    A. It rains
    B. Clouds form in the sky
    C. It snows
    D. The heat gets worse

18. **The psychologist testified that the defendant had what?**
    A. Homicidal tendencies
    B. Schizophrenia
    C. A learning disability
    D. Nothing wrong with him

19. **In order to vote 'not guilty' a juror must believe what?**
   A. The defendant is not guilty
   B. The defendant does not deserve to die
   C. There is reasonable doubt
   D. The defendant had an unfair trial

20. **Who directed the 1957 film version?**
   A. George Stevens
   B. Elia Kazan
   C. Billy Wilder
   D. Syndey Lumet

21. **What point is proved at the end of Act I?**
   A. The old man couldn't have seen the boy run down the stairs
   B. The woman could not have recognized the boy
   C. The knives were not identical
   D. People don't always mean exactly what they say

22. **Who do the jurors posit the woman wasn't wearing glasses in court?**
   A. Vanity
   B. They had broken
   C. They would discredit her testimony
   D. Headaches

23. **The defendant reminds the 3rd juror of whom?**
   A. His son
   B. His boss
   C. His uncle
   D. His father

24. **Which juror wears glasses (according to the script?)**
   A. 3rd Juror
   B. 4th Juror
   C. 8th Juror
   D. 9th Juror

25. Which juror changes his vote just to get deliberations over with?

A. 3rd Juror
B. 7th Juror
C. 9th Juror
D. 12th Juror

Quiz 3 Answer Key

1. **(C)** Advertising agent
2. **(C)** Kid
3. **(C)** A cold
4. **(C)** A teleplay
5. **(D)** They are a 'hung jury'
6. **(B)** They had a fight, and the victim (his father) struck him
7. **(C)** 15 seconds
8. **(C)** His sleeve is torn
9. **(D)** New York City
10. **(C)** Television
11. **(A)** Social issues
12. **(D)** 2004
13. **(B)** 1957
14. **(C)** Henry Fonda
15. **(B)** Jack Lemmon
16. **(C)** Naturalism
17. **(A)** It rains
18. **(A)** Homicidal tendencies
19. **(C)** There is reasonable doubt
20. **(D)** Syndey Lumet
21. **(D)** People don't always mean exactly what they say
22. **(A)** Vanity
23. **(A)** His son
24. **(B)** 4th Juror
25. **(B)** 7th Juror

Quiz 4

1. **During the second vote, when 8th Juror abstains, who decides to continue deliberations by voting 'not guilty?'**
   A. Foreman
   B. 5th Juror
   C. 9th Juror
   D. 10th Juror

2. **Which juror questions whether or not the defendant would have returned to the scene after killing his father?**
   A. 4th Juror
   B. 8th Juror
   C. 11th Juror
   D. 12th Juror

3. **How many settings does this play have?**
   A. 1
   B. 2
   C. 3
   D. 5

4. **Why does 3rd Juror say that 5th Juror changes his vote?**
   A. He wants to get deliberations over
   B. Because he sympathizes with the kid, having grown up in the slum
   C. He is stupid
   D. He is persuaded by 8th Juror

5. **8th Juror tests the memory of which juror to prove a point?**
   A. 4th Juror
   B. 7th Juror
   C. 9th Juror
   D. 10th Juror

6. **Which juror illustrates how to use a switchblade correctly?**
   A. 3rd Juror
   B. 5th Juror
   C. 8th Juror
   D. 10th Juror

7. **Which is the only juror to change his vote more than once?**
   A. Foreman
   B. 7th Juror
   C. 9th Juror
   D. 12th Juror

8. **8th Juror tests the memory of which juror to prove a point?**
   A. 4th Juror
   B. 7th Juror
   C. 9th Juror
   D. 10th Juror

9. **What is 10th Juror's occupation?**
   A. Lawyer
   B. Preacher
   C. Actor
   D. Garage owner

10. **What is 7th Juror's occupation?**
    A. Fireman
    B. Florist
    C. Salesman
    D. Journalist

11. **What is 2nd Juror's occupation?**
    A. Teacher
    B. Mailman
    C. Police officer
    D. Bank clerk

12. **On what network did 12 Angry Men, the teleplay, originally premiere?**
    A. ABC
    B. NBC
    C. CBS
    D. PBS

13. **What sports team was 7th Juror trying to see that evening?**
    A. Giants
    B. Yankees
    C. Mets
    D. Nets

14. **Who is the main protagonist of the play?**
    A. Foreman
    B. 7th Juror
    C. 8th Juror
    D. 12th Juror

15. **Who is the main antagonist of the play?**
    A. 2nd Juror
    B. 3rd Juror
    C. 10th Juror
    D. 11th Juror

16. **How did the jurors figure out how long it would take the old man to get to his door?**
    A. They watched video evidence
    B. They brought the old man back in
    C. They simulated it
    D. They guessed

17. **Why don't the jurors originally believe the defendant's testimony?**
    A. He is unable to produce a ticket stub
    B. Friends testify that he was with them when the movie began
    C. People at the movies testify to not remembering him there
    D. He can't remember the names of the movies

18. **Who is responsible for proving the facts of the case?**
    A. The defendant
    B. The prosecutor
    C. The judge
    D. The jurors

19. **What do most jurors believe when they enter the jury room?**
    A. The defending lawyer was very good
    B. The victim was a bad man
    C. The defendant is guilty
    D. The judge was particularly mean

20. **Who is not a witness in the case?**
    A. The defendant's friend
    B. The father
    C. The across-the-street neighbor
    D. The downstairs neighbor

21. **What word(s) describes having thought about a crime beforehand?**
    A. Murder
    B. Premeditated
    C. Manslaughter
    D. 2nd Degree

22. **What does the prosecution prove about the across-the-street neighbor's ability to act as an eyewitness?**
    A. She was wearing her glasses
    B. She could see through the El Train windows
    C. She did not know the boy or his father
    D. She has a strong memory

23. **What is the outcome of the trial?**
    A. Guilty
    B. The play ends with deliberations ongoing
    C. Hung jury
    D. Not guilty

24. **Where was the victim's body while the defendant was being questioned?**
    A. Missing
    B. Next door
    C. Downstairs
    D. In the morgue

25. **What about the defendant's past leads them to believe that he killed the victim?**
    A. A debt problem
    B. A history of mental illness
    C. A violent temper
    D. A criminal record

Quiz 4 Answer Key

1. **(C)** 9th Juror
2. **(C)** 11th Juror
3. **(A)** 1
4. **(B)** Because he sympathizes with the kid, having grown up in the slum
5. **(A)** 4th Juror
6. **(B)** 5th Juror
7. **(D)** 12th Juror
8. **(A)** 4th Juror
9. **(D)** Garage owner
10. **(C)** Salesman
11. **(D)** Bank clerk
12. **(C)** CBS
13. **(B)** Yankees
14. **(C)** 8th Juror
15. **(B)** 3rd Juror
16. **(C)** They simulated it
17. **(D)** He can't remember the names of the movies
18. **(B)** The prosecutor
19. **(C)** The defendant is guilty
20. **(B)** The father
21. **(B)** Premeditated
22. **(B)** She could see through the El Train windows
23. **(D)** Not guilty
24. **(B)** Next door
25. **(D)** A criminal record

ClassicNotes

GradeSaver™

Getting you the grade since 1999™

Other ClassicNotes from GradeSaver™

12 Angry Men
1984
A&P and Other Stories
Absalom, Absalom
Adam Bede
The Adventures of Augie March
The Adventures of Huckleberry Finn
The Adventures of Tom Sawyer
The Aeneid
Agamemnon
The Age of Innocence
The Alchemist (Coelho)
The Alchemist (Jonson)
Alice in Wonderland
All My Sons
All Quiet on the Western Front
All the King's Men
All the Pretty Horses
Allen Ginsberg's Poetry
The Ambassadors
American Beauty
And Then There Were None
Angela's Ashes
Animal Farm
Anna Karenina
Anthem
Antigone
Antony and Cleopatra
Aristotle's Poetics
Aristotle's Politics

Aristotle: Nicomachean Ethics
As I Lay Dying
As You Like It
Astrophil and Stella
Atlas Shrugged
Atonement
The Awakening
Babbitt
The Bacchae
Bartleby the Scrivener
The Bean Trees
The Bell Jar
Beloved
Benito Cereno
Beowulf
Bhagavad-Gita
Billy Budd
Black Boy
Bleak House
Bless Me, Ultima
Blindness
Blood Wedding
The Bloody Chamber
Bluest Eye
The Bonfire of the Vanities
The Book of Daniel
The Book of the Duchess and Other Poems
The Book Thief
Brave New World
Breakfast at Tiffany's
Breakfast of Champions
The Brief Wondrous Life of Oscar Wao

The Brothers Karamazov
The Burning Plain and Other Stories
A Burnt-Out Case
By Night in Chile
Call of the Wild
Candide
The Canterbury Tales
Cat on a Hot Tin Roof
Cat's Cradle
Catch-22
The Catcher in the Rye
Cathedral
The Caucasian Chalk Circle
Charlotte Temple
Charlotte's Web
The Cherry Orchard
The Chocolate War
The Chosen
A Christmas Carol
Christopher Marlowe's Poems
Chronicle of a Death Foretold
Civil Disobedience
Civilization and Its Discontents
A Clockwork Orange
Coleridge's Poems
The Color of Water
The Color Purple
Comedy of Errors
Communist Manifesto
A Confederacy of Dunces

For our full list of over 250 Study Guides, Quizzes,
Sample College Application Essays, Literature Essays and E-texts, visit:

www.gradesaver.com

ClassicNotes

GrAdeSaver™

Getting you the grade since 1999™

Other ClassicNotes from GradeSaver™

Confessions
Confessions of an
    English Opium Eater
Connecticut Yankee in
    King Arthur's Court
The Consolation of
    Philosophy
Coriolanus
The Count of Monte
    Cristo
The Country Wife
Crime and Punishment
The Crucible
Cry, the Beloved
    Country
The Crying of Lot 49
The Curious Incident of
    the Dog in the
    Night-time
Cymbeline
Daisy Miller
David Copperfield
Death in Venice
Death of a Salesman
The Death of Ivan Ilych
Democracy in America
Devil in a Blue Dress
Dharma Bums
The Diary of a Young
    Girl by Anne Frank
Disgrace
Divine Comedy-I:
    Inferno
Do Androids Dream of
    Electric Sheep?

Doctor Faustus
    (Marlowe)
A Doll's House
Don Quixote Book I
Don Quixote Book II
Dora: An Analysis of a
    Case of Hysteria
Dr. Jekyll and Mr. Hyde
Dracula
Dubliners
The Duchess of Malfi
East of Eden
Electra by Sophocles
The Electric Kool-Aid
    Acid Test
Emily Dickinson's
    Collected Poems
Emma
Ender's Game
Endgame
The English Patient
The Epic of Gilgamesh
Ethan Frome
The Eumenides
Everyman: Morality Play
Everything is Illuminated
The Faerie Queene
Fahrenheit 451
The Fall of the House of
    Usher
A Farewell to Arms
The Federalist Papers
Fences
Fight Club
Fight Club (Film)
Flags of Our Fathers

Flannery O'Connor's
    Stories
For Whom the Bell Tolls
The Fountainhead
Frankenstein
Franny and Zooey
The Giver
The Glass Castle
The Glass Menagerie
The God of Small Things
Goethe's Faust
The Good Earth
The Good Woman of
    Setzuan
The Grapes of Wrath
Great Expectations
The Great Gatsby
Grendel
The Guest
Gulliver's Travels
Hamlet
The Handmaid's Tale
Hard Times
Haroun and the Sea of
    Stories
Harry Potter and the
    Philosopher's Stone
Heart of Darkness
Hedda Gabler
Henry IV (Pirandello)
Henry IV Part 1
Henry IV Part 2
Henry V
Herzog
Hippolytus
The Hobbit

For our full list of over 250 Study Guides, Quizzes,
Sample College Application Essays, Literature Essays and E-texts, visit:

www.gradesaver.com

ClassicNotes

GrⲀdeSaver™

Getting you the grade since 1999™

Other ClassicNotes from GradeSaver™

A Midsummer Night's Dream
The Mill on the Floss
Moby Dick
A Modest Proposal and Other Satires
Moll Flanders
The Most Dangerous Game
Mother Courage and Her Children
Mrs. Dalloway
Much Ado About Nothing
My Antonia
Mythology
The Namesake
Narrative of the Life of Frederick Douglass, An American Slave: Written by Himself
Native Son
Never Let Me Go
Nickel and Dimed: On (Not) Getting By in America
Night
Nine Stories
No Exit
Northanger Abbey
Notes from Underground
O Pioneers
The Odyssey
Oedipus Rex or Oedipus the King
Of Mice and Men

The Old Man and the Sea
Oliver Twist
On Liberty
On the Road
One Day in the Life of Ivan Denisovich
One Flew Over the Cuckoo's Nest
One Hundred Years of Solitude
Oroonoko
Oryx and Crake
Othello
Our Town
The Outsiders
Pale Fire
Pamela: Or Virtue Rewarded
Paradise Lost
A Passage to India
The Pearl
Percy Shelley: Poems
Perfume: The Story of a Murderer
Persepolis: The Story of a Childhood
Persuasion
Phaedra
Phaedrus
The Piano Lesson
The Picture of Dorian Gray
Poe's Poetry
Poe's Short Stories
Poems of W.B. Yeats: The Rose

Poems of W.B. Yeats: The Tower
The Poems of William Blake
The Poisonwood Bible
Pope's Poems and Prose
Portrait of the Artist as a Young Man
The Praise of Folly
Pride and Prejudice
The Prince
The Professor's House
Prometheus Bound
Pudd'nhead Wilson
Purple Hibiscus
Pygmalion
Rabbit, Run
A Raisin in the Sun
The Real Life of Sebastian Knight
Rebecca
The Red Badge of Courage
The Remains of the Day
The Republic
Rhinoceros
Richard II
Richard III
The Rime of the Ancient Mariner
Rip Van Winkle and Other Stories
The Road
Robert Frost: Poems
Robinson Crusoe

For our full list of over 250 Study Guides, Quizzes,
Sample College Application Essays, Literature Essays and E-texts, visit:

www.gradesaver.com

ClassicNotes

Gr**A**deSaver™

Getting you the grade since 1999™

Other ClassicNotes from GradeSaver™

Roll of Thunder, Hear
  My Cry
Romeo and Juliet
A Room of One's Own
A Room With a View
A Rose For Emily and
  Other Short Stories
Rosencrantz and
  Guildenstern Are
  Dead
Salome
The Scarlet Letter
The Scarlet Pimpernel
The Seagull
Season of Migration to
  the North
Second Treatise of
  Government
The Secret Life of Bees
The Secret River
Secret Sharer
Sense and Sensibility
A Separate Peace
Shakespeare's Sonnets
Shantaram
She Stoops to Conquer
Short Stories of Ernest
  Hemingway
Short Stories of F. Scott
  Fitzgerald
Siddhartha
Silas Marner
Sir Gawain and the
  Green Knight
Sir Thomas Wyatt:
  Poems

Sister Carrie
Six Characters in Search
  of an Author
Slaughterhouse Five
Snow Falling on Cedars
The Social Contract
Something Wicked This
  Way Comes
Song of Roland
Song of Solomon
Songs of Innocence and
  of Experience
Sons and Lovers
The Sorrows of Young
  Werther
The Sound and the Fury
The Sound of Waves
The Spanish Tragedy
Spenser's Amoretti and
  Epithalamion
Spring Awakening
The Stranger
A Streetcar Named
  Desire
A Study in Scarlet
Sula
The Sun Also Rises
Sundiata: An Epic of Old
  Mali
Tale of Two Cities
The Taming of the Shrew
The Tempest
Tender is the Night
Tess of the D'Urbervilles
Their Eyes Were
  Watching God

Things Fall Apart
The Things They Carried
A Thousand Splendid
  Suns
The Threepenny Opera
Through the Looking
  Glass
Thus Spoke Zarathustra
The Time Machine
Titus Andronicus
To Build a Fire
To Kill a Mockingbird
To the Lighthouse
The Tortilla Curtain
Touching Spirit Bear
Treasure Island
Trifles
Troilus and Cressida
Tropic of Cancer
Tropic of Capricorn
Tuesdays With Morrie
The Turn of the Screw
Twelfth Night
Twilight
Ulysses
Uncle Tom's Cabin
Utopia
Vanity Fair
A Very Old Man With
  Enormous Wings
Villette
A Vindication of the
  Rights of Woman
The Visit
Volpone
Waiting for Godot

For our full list of over 250 Study Guides, Quizzes,
Sample College Application Essays, Literature Essays and E-texts, visit:

www.gradesaver.com

ClassicNotes

GradeSaver™

Getting you the grade since 1999™

For our full list of over 250 Study Guides, Quizzes,
Sample College Application Essays, Literature Essays and E-texts, visit:

www.gradesaver.com

21392333R00048

Made in the USA
Middletown, DE
27 June 2015